Insomnia

Arun M Sivakrishna

India | USA | UK

Copyright © Arun M Sivakrishna
All Rights Reserved.

This book has been self-published with all reasonable efforts taken to make the material error-free by the author. No part of this book shall be used, reproduced in any manner whatsoever without written permission from the author, except in the case of brief quotations embodied in critical articles and reviews.

The Author of this book is solely responsible and liable for its content including but not limited to the views, representations, descriptions, statements, information, opinions, and references ["Content"]. The Content of this book shall not constitute or be construed or deemed to reflect the opinion or expression of the Publisher or Editor. Neither the Publisher nor Editor endorse or approve the Content of this book or guarantee the reliability, accuracy, or completeness of the Content published herein and do not make any representations or warranties of any kind, express or implied, including but not limited to the implied warranties of merchantability, fitness for a particular purpose.

The Publisher and Editor shall not be liable whatsoever...

Made with ❤ on the BookLeaf Publishing Platform
www.bookleafpub.in
www.bookleafpub.com

Dedication

Dedicated to all those who carried a storm within,
please remember, even silence sings.

Preface

Acknowledgements

My first collection, *Songs of a Solitary Tree*, came out in November 2014.

In the eleven years that have passed, the act of writing has been rare—a fleeting thought on a sticky note here, a nameless verse there. Despite this erratic quiet, a few cherished people have never stopped encouraging me to give voice to the emotions. This is a message for them, a small acknowledgment of their faith.

If you are one of them, I hope this makes you smile

1. When We are Gone

Then,
we would come across in
someone's dreams, like how
strangers often meet, thinking
we might know this person
somehow somewhere,
so familiar, yet could not
pin on who could this be.

Smiling politely we
go our ways, carrying
perhaps some morsels of
unidentified memories,
all the while tapping to the
tunes of the songs
we once shared.

Familiar strangers
hum the same song,
each to own tunes.

2. Nobody Remains Citizens

The day, mom got knocked over
by a speeding motorist,
she was getting newly prescribed nephro pills
for dad from a pharmacy offering ten percent
discount on the printed rates.

As she was taken to the
hospital nearby in a fishtailing rickshaw,
all she had asked was to
take her home instead, to the man
she kept in a recliner, in an unlocked front room,
eyes fixed at the gate, eagerly
waiting for her arrival back.

That, now he no longer is there and
she often walks unsteadily doesnt matter,
so long as she could make it back that day
to a helpless old man, soaked in his own piss with
not even a dog beside him to lick him off his woes.

Someone always leaves home,
to work, learn, pick the kids from school,
to get rations, to stand in serpentine queues
for the dolled out welfares, perhaps to get medicines
from Janoushadi where they offer ten rupees less.

Someone leaves home, to protest,
some protest against protests,
some, riot and hurl petrol bombs where
hordes of cops turn around, look elsewhere
like guards scanning soccer gallery
while the last of the spot kicks were taken and a
lone keeper leaps to block the cannon at his post.

Somebody leaving home arent just citizens
with random UID numbers, or corpses in morgues
with tags tied around toes, fragmented limbs
waiting for matching DNAs to take them home to.

There is always some one, for all the departed,
waiting behind, writhing in pain
seething in anger to tell you that
Nobody remains, just a citizen anymore.

3. Maps

Geography never was
my high point. Rather
making histories with
ever changing cartographies
of the worlds I moved about,
taking along the asterisk pinned
"You Are Here" in sheaf and
sheets of maps mostly redrawn
stashed away, after ceding territories in
wars waged in rage and of retreats in haste.

Each of those grids,
star dusts,
rubicon fritters,
the points of
no return still remind,
about chords snapped,
umbilical and all such,
the trenches around borders,
barbed fences cutting through

torso, while crawling back across
and then, perhaps
the ominous boom of the stock
when the bullet traverses a free way
through the heart.

You are now,
neither a twinkling star
nor a blooming flower.
Just a blob of red and a
leaking faucet of myriad hues.

4. Unfinished

We were crossing a stream,
high up in the misty hills,
yet another of his obsessions.
Shaky plank, pale reminder,
of the bridge it used to be.
He stopped in the middle,
swaying, side to side,
looked funny, humming a
lilting tune only he could hear and
thrown at me, more as a challenge,
"The other side is rebirth, if you make it over",
I swallowed a cuss word.
"But, its one too many" and he stepped into the abyss.
Laughter echoing down the nadirs of the
endless pit of an unforgettable dream.
Garlanded face in the wall,
grinning back,
"got you".
I Couldnt sleep afterwards.

5. Ticket to a round trip of Guilt

The new one there,
he picked on a
rare day of escapade,
who sailed along to
heavens unseen before,
was once a wife too,
a virtuous one at that,
a doting mother and dutiful daughter,
in a not too distant past, in a
village by the hills, rain forests and meandering streams.

The happy pictures,
snippets of an incarnation past,
of celebrations and revelries,
an infant making baby steps,
a toothless face beaming,
birthday boy flanked by proud parents,
aren't sort of illusions she keeps,
but remnants of a world, disappeared suddenly that

swept her off in a ravaging deluge.

Gone,
the euphoria of peaks scaled,
in place, an emptiness,
and with it, stashes of
free tickets to all the guilt trips,
he never thought of ever riding on.

Does it help,
that he was gentle as she said?
The coupons and
few extra bills he insisted,
make him a Budha of sorts?

6. Seasons : Summer

We ran in
from the sweltering heat of the beach
to the cool cocoon
of our space in the dingy inn.

Shed clothes like children,
strolled hand in hand,
exploring uninhabited corners
of the cosy little island
we gladly marooned ourselves in.

Skipping, tripping,
we tumbled —
the rug became our sea.
We swam through swells,
surfed soft crests,
slipped and slid into wetlands.

Slithering like tangled snakes,
rustling through fallen leaves,

hissing and kissing,
we coiled into the valley.

Morphed into colt and mare,
set the meadows on fire.
Neighing wild, we galloped
neck to neck,
racing flags,
crashing into each other
as Vega rose in the east
beneath a cerulean summer sky.

7. Seasons : Monsoon

My love,
It's been raining awhile here,
and I am all alone, sitting by the window,
watching the copious tears
this gloomy sky keeps shedding.

It was exactly the same, then too—
I remember
you slipping through the archway,
reluctantly leaving me
in a still-pouring rain,
to an impatient cab.

The image of you, looking through the side pane,
dissolving into frescos
by the dripping droplets—
that's all the memory I have of you now,
and it's never left me
for a moment since.

Memories can be cruel;
they take away the best,
yet play only the painful ones,
pounding a hapless heart
into untold miseries.

Sometimes, in the sleepless travails
through unknown realms of apparitions,
I feel you beside me—
tracing the lobes and folds,
peaks and valleys,
rising and falling like a brook—
and I curl to the side
where you used to be,
a leg clasped over mine.

Often, I go back in time,
frame by frame,
trying to stitch the rebus fragments
to the point where it all began,
to relive the magic
we had woven together.

But there is no crossing back from Rubicons and
a forlorn face alone
is mine to keep now.

8. Seasons : Autumn and after

Like foliage of woods
alter hues in autumn,
my memories of you too
turn grey before they wither away.
A deciduous tree, I stand
stripped off all that is once green and tender.

Flock of birds fled to
farther shores we never been to,
taking along, the songs we crooned together,
leaving stanzas of silence in our duets now.
Perhaps this is what time does,
can't say, quite sudden and unannounced,
a slow descent, I confess.

Like seeped out rainbows
in monochromed horizons,
all that once burned bright

now lies muted, dull and pale.

I sense it is going to be winter here,
long and unforgiving.
Each day, it sleets on the
frozen sea between us,
trapping beneath, entombed
a thousand shipwrecked memories
we have of each other.

9. Seasons : Spring

I've lost all track of time—
can't tell if it's day or night,
weeks or eons passed.
Memory has gone blank.
How we arrived here?

All around me:
a world swathed in flawless white—
thick, silent, suffocating.
The pain returns, sharp but nameless—
perhaps because sorrow
breathes through festering reminders,
invisible yet everywhere.

I stopped shoveling snow long ago.
Let it pile high,
block every threshold,
seal every exit.
Now I wait—
for avalanche:

to bury me whole,
or sweep the wreckage clean.

But I feel it coming.
Change.
Not distant—near.
Already stirring.

It strikes when least expected:
walking home late, half-asleep,
through alley-mazes to the lonely room;
or swaying on the Tube,
gripping cold metal,
surrounded by faces just as hollow;
or drowning sorrows
in cheap whiskey at some forgotten bar—
then,
a surge inside.
a longing so fierce
it stitches every wound,
melts every frost.

And then—
an entire valley,
bursting into bloom.

It is Spring.

Not just season,
but resurrection,
the quiet return
of hope.

10. Defrost

Now you see
it has become very cold here between us.
Fine flakes of snow turning into ice,
forming an impregnable wall of silence.

Do you know,
if you stay cold to the touch,
will have frost bite and gangrene?

A strip of ice, makes nothing grow over,
no flowers bloom, no birds ever sing,
only frosted memories get buried under.

Think of it,
the stars we see now are of the same sky
the sultry night, still the same.
Sweltering heat and
the sweat beads on us,
though we are a world apart,
are of the same garland.

Come over,
croon sweet nothings
punctuated with kisses.

11. Afterglow

When it's all over, all you take home is a frozen frame of rheumy eyes, half-closed, etched in silence.
Someday — perhaps not soon — it will be on you, like dried flowers crumbling between pages of a long-forgotten book.

You may buckle. Grip a banister. A chair. Sink to the floor. Curl up like a question mark.

A lump will rise — sudden, suffocating. Breath stolen by memory's tide.
Then — the breaking open. Anguish, raw and tidal.

And after the storm? The void remains. Not empty — *enormous.*

It doesn't swallow you at once. It kills you moment by moment, stealing the shape of days until nothing fits the way it did.

What was once bliss — the brightest light — now triggers
the floodgates. Each face you pass holds a ghost of theirs.
Every ping. Every song. In dreams, in dishes, in
brushstrokes, in traffic, that faint sketch of a smile
haunts, lingers, refuses to fade.

So you try to rebuild. Keep tissues nearby, not for tears,
but to sculpt a face, Stretch sinew. Pull skin taut.
Adjust shadows. Correct tones. Make. Break. Remake.
Until, one day, a face emerges.
Not perfect. Not whole But *there it for sure.*

Pray it makes you smile. If it doesn't, nothing, I swear,
nothing will be more terrible than that.

The sun went down in crimson pool.
A palette of red stayed afloat,
unclaimed,
unfading,
unfinished.

12. Hibernation

It's winter now.
A sea of flaking white,
only Mahonias and Jacquelines bloom bright,
just as you loved them.

Of flowers,
I'd rather you be a wreath upon my chest
than a lonely rose pinned to a lapel.

The last time we walked this aisle,
you were already like a blossom cut too soon —
yet smiling, solemn,
cradled in a bed of white roses.

Now, on the day I take my final stride down this same path —
the one I've avoided since —
let me go with you, riding my own tide.

I'll stare through the drone of sermons,

hard into the stars,
until they blink,
until they implode,
and the sky forgets to hold them.

Then, gladly,
we'll slip beneath —
into the hush of that named burrow,
where no season dares follow.

13. Sea, star and you by my side

On a starlit night
by the beach, when the
ocean slapped the wall we sat on,
I fell on my back
into the rising swell
and when the receding waves
drew me farther into the sea
a meteor arched high across
and your face sparkled
in a flurry of flares.

I haven't seen you since

14. Size Does Matter

Lassie was busy collecting.
Been everywhere in the neighborhood
bringing robes of all kind.
Kiddo's, boys', gals',
the momma stuff and for the
grand elders even.

Sorting, marking, labelling,
some to the laundrette
with my number on the tags and
" dont forget to pick'em on your way back" texts.

No one was spared,
Mom, parted with some sweaters,
bro, a stack of denims and tees.
Curious, why she never came to me,
pat came the reply, "dad, which poor
soul could possibly fit into yours?
They would mostly be skinny !"

15. Jinxed

"The night you were born",
mom started again,
after another spell of the
now familiar silence.
" I was screaming in pain the whole day".

" Perhaps, it was jinxed" I told her,
offering no comfort whatsoever.

" In hindsight, absolutely.
Torrential rains and bolts.
spiteful lightnings, were the only light
in that trembling ward".

Staring through her, i nudged
"No cows died, as legends say
when demons are born? "

She paused and considered,
Whispered softly and I had to lean in to her to pick that

" Your grandma,
lost two of her
finest, both to snakes and cried out,
Oh Child, you brought
home quite a handful this time"

16. Diary Of A Dervish

15-12-2014

Dear Diary,
It was fun the whole evening
though towards the end, I puked as
my head was reeling bad.
So much I swirled to get that twirl right,
the way it was shown at school today.

Nana said, I look funny in the Tennure*
ammi cut and sewn out of Abba's white tunic.
But Abba smiled, adjusted his cap into a *Sikke***,
placed it on my head and said
"You look fine."

16-12-2014

Dear Diary,
Aman giggled, when he saw my sikke,
His uncle brought one from Lebanon,

woven camel hair, soft as a prayer.

Shaheedji, our master told us of
Darwish Mahmoud***, and set one of his verses
to a pristine, solemn chant, it was one of his best
that he had picked to set it to a chant
It was pristine, piercing and made us a bit sad too.

But once we started, we were lost in it
Remember Shaheedji smiling and
Aman's face had an ethereal glow.
Guess, he had tears in his eyes
"Oh Father, my brother neither love nor
want me in their midst" and I saw
Aman falling, swirling round and
round and round, squirting
blobs of reds all across.

Others too, Sama, Khalid, Masterji, Ruhan, Ishmeil.

My knees, suddenly gave away and
I too fell, like a Tennure falling in heaps.
Couldn't feel anything anymore
But I know I can dance no more

17-12-2014

Dear Diary,

132 and still to go
" Oh Father, my brother neither love nor
Want me in their midst"****

In memory of the innocent children who lost their lives in Peshawar school massacre on 16 Dec 14.

*Tennure : The wide white skirt, a Dervish wear, a symbol of Ego's shroud
** Sikke : A Camel's hair hat, represents tombstone of the ego.
***Darwish Mahmoud, a Palestinian poet, (13 March 1941- 9 Aug 2008)
**** lines are from Darwish Mahmoud's " I am Yousuf, Oh my Father".

17. Lost And Found

Every heart has serrations,
unique in a way
no two fingers have
the same prints.

Memories,
perhaps, like punched
keys, open the lock
which matches the grooves.

A brittle leaf, in a
book since untouched
suddenly opens a chamber
and, it bleeds again
from a wound that hasn't healed.

A feather, turquoise
with still the eye intact,
pleads to key in the digits to
listen to a voice that

trailed off in a raging storm.

Tele is in the din, but
a chord rises unbidden,
you hum along wondering why
that lyric still clings like a
ghost who forgot to leave.

18. Where Ghosts Still Lurk

Nothing ever leaves
without residue.

Limbs severed still ache—
phantom limbs, twitching,
itching ghosts of those flesh
once grafted to an unsuspecting trunk.

In sleepless hours,
you reach for the ring
on a finger crossed out in red—
from a hand long left the clasp and
taste supple lips which
no longer seek yours,

When crows — a murder of them —
caw, caw in delirious pitch,
in a frantic urge, still
you still sneak in and nuzzle into a
familiar warmth, a ghost now left.

A shoulder, a sigh, a name whispered at dawn.

Phantom limbs.
Phantom pains.

Nothing stays.
Nothing simply leaves.
It haunts.
It hums.
It waits in the marrow.

19. A Friend In Weed Is A ...

Last time,
high on weed and tongue loose,
I blurted: *I fancy your wife.*

He kissed my squeaky pate,
laughed soft through smoke:
"What's mine is yours too."

That night,
rain slashing like open wounds,
we carried him between us,
she shouting *"Hurry, hurry!"*
as I stumbled over a dried-up stump,
nearly dropped him in the mud.

Almost dawn.
We carved space in the storm,
heaving earth under thunder's roar.

She took over then,

kneeling, gentle, precise,
while I lit one last joint
and watched, awed,
by the rhythm of her grace.

Before she could finish,
an angry gust tore through,
ripped the sheet from his face.

There,
eyes still open,
searching mine:
But why?

She didn't flinch.
Tipped the barrow high, over his
still-smiling face
just how it was,
before the skull took the blow.

20. Scented Memories

On this lazy Sunday,
while the rest nurse sore eyes
and silence their alarms,
I wander the winding lanes
where memories lie like strewn blossoms,
some faded, some still blooming along hedgerows
where a beaming face often used to wait,
with gooseberries and salt-laced mangoes,
wildflowers tucked shyly behind her ear.

I still see them,
those green-ribboned plaits,
one always slipping forward,
crowned with jasmine buds.
"Oh, Mother clips them in," she'd say,
"to keep the lice away."

Another frame surges now,
the stone steps sloping to the pond,
where a boy of ten sat one step lower,

squinting up as twilight draped her
in an amber glow,
and she sang—soft, uncertain—
a keertan newly learned.

I hum it still,
over a peg or two,
when the glass is low
and the light leans gold again.

21. Happy Women's day

Not to lag behind,
I posted it bright and early:
Photo: Me + Wife + Daughter
Caption: *"Two women in my life."*
#HappyWomensDay #Blessed

"Call for you!" — the little one sang out.
Mom, on the line, voice crackling static:
*"What — so me and your sister
mean nothing to you?"*
Deleted. Rewrote. Reposted:
"The Four Women In My Life."

"Call for you," smirked the wife —
old password, new venom, ever on stage,
whispering like a seething villain
"Oh. So it was never how I thought."

Then — melee.
Aunties, classmates, "Glass mates."

In-laws. Outlaws. Cousins twice-removed-by-choice.
Comments flooded like monsoon drains:
"Why? Don't we mean anything??"
"Unfollowed."
"This is why men shouldn't post."

I pulled the plug. Logged out.
Sat in digital silence.
Peace? Not even close.
Because now
it's *their* turn.

The Four Women In My Life
circling like justices of the peace
demanding answers on
"Why the post was removed?

www.ingramcontent.com/pod-product-compliance
Lightning Source LLC
Chambersburg PA
CBHW070039070426
42449CB00012BA/3097